Questions
that Help a Relationship

by Shakeena Jefferson

DORRANCE
PUBLISHING CO
EST. 1920
PITTSBURGH, PENNSYLVANIA 15238

The contents of this work, including, but not limited to, the accuracy of events, people, and places depicted; opinions expressed; permission to use previously published materials included; and any advice given or actions advocated are solely the responsibility of the author, who assumes all liability for said work and indemnifies the publisher against any claims stemming from publication of the work.

Dorrance Publishing Co
585 Alpha Drive, Suite 103
Pittsburgh, PA 15238
Visit our website at *www.dorrancebookstore.com*

ISBN: 978-1-4809-1923-5
eISBN: 978-1-4809-1900-6

Contents

Chapter 1

Why Do People Begin to Think They're Unattractive in a Relationship?

Sometimes in a relationship, there is one who feels the other has stopped paying attention to them like they used to. Even though that might not be the case, in the person's head, that is the thought that has registered. Some people may think they're unattractive in a relationship because they change over time. Their bodies may have changed and they feel they look different. The other person may turn their head when another male or female walks past and shows them attention.

There may be one who feels the other should have low self-esteem so they will think they are unattractive. One also could have had a bad last relationship, where the other made them believe they were unattractive when they really weren't. Why would someone make a person feel this way, you ask? Insecurities. Their childhood may have brought on these insecure feelings.

Maybe they felt unwanted and unloved, but now that they're older, they plan on never feeling this way again. One may feel the other only wants them around for one specific thing and that they don't really care about them at all. Loneliness is what usually brings this feeling on. If your significant other is always gone and doesn't really want you to leave the house, this idea may begin to form in your mind.

One may feel that the other thinks they are unattractive because they don't have sexual activity with them anymore. The person may also begin to think they are unattractive because their mind is telling them their significant other is cheating on them. In some situations, a couple may have sexual intercourse most of the time, but then one begins to feel that is all the other cares about. Sometimes people get these feelings, and usually they trust them; even though sometimes they may be wrong, at times they can be right also.

Somebody else comes into the picture and their self-esteem gets low. If somebody else comes into the picture, of course the significant other would get upset because it is obvious that their person is paying attention to them. In the beginning, one may feel they got more compliments, but then they realize the compliments have gone away. It makes some people feel good to hear that they look good from their significant other.

If they actually hear the words being said to them, they will know they are attractive. One may feel they're significant other doesn't spend time with them. Everyone adores attention; if they feel they are not getting enough, some hurt feelings may develop. Some people may begin to think they are unattractive because they know the spark in their relationship has gone away.

Usually when people feel the spark is gone in their relationship, they know it won't be long before the relationship is over, but they try to hang in there anyway. Some people in a relationship may feel they're not getting enough attention. Even though the person's significant other may be around, the person might still feel neglected if they feel the person's attention is not on them all the time. The person may also think they don't look good enough.

Since the person already feels ignored and neglected, they may begin to think they don't look good enough to get their significant other's attention. Some people may begin to think they are unattractive because the sex in their relationship is not good. Obviously since they are not enjoying the sex with their significant other, they feel they are not enjoying it, either. They feel if there is no sexual attraction, there is no other kind of attraction, either.

A person may begin to think they are unattractive because they have gained weight. They may feel their person has started seeing them differently because they are not as fit and slim as they were when they first met. The person may begin to think they're unattractive in a relationship because of the way they carry themselves. If someone in a relationship already thinks they don't look good, they may get to thinking, *What does it matter if I dress up or not?*

Some may begin to think they are unattractive in a relationship because they start to see the real person they are dating and they notice things they didn't notice before. It is like Jekyll and Hyde; maybe the person was all nice and sweet one second, and the next was bad, wild, and out of control. Some people may begin to feel they are unattractive in a relationship because they have low self-esteem already and they get in a relationship in which the other person puts them down by disliking what they do. In some cases, a person may do everything they possibly can plus more to impress their significant other in a relationship.

Even after they do all they can, sometimes they look and realize it's still not good enough. Finally they start to realize the attraction that was once there in their relationship may have gone away. The unattractive feelings could also come because their partner changes their attitude toward them. When someone first meets someone they are attracted to, they go all out trying to please the person and keep them happy.

But later on, if their partner shows no interest and doesn't care whether they are happy or not, they will feel like they are nothing other than the old ball and chain. The person may feel their partner has stopped recognizing small things about them. It doesn't have to be much; it could be that their partner used to tell them they had a pretty smile or finished their sentences for them. The point is no matter how small, it meant a lot to the person because you did it at all.

Some people may begin to think they're unattractive in a relationship because of things that happened before they got in the relationship. Also, because the other person may not be keeping things the same. Even though the person may care about their significant other, they have trouble showing it because of insecure feelings. These feelings can come from many things, but they usually come from a feeling of neglect or from being hurt before.

Usually people in a relationship like to switch things up so they won't become boring, but sometimes people like to keep things the same. Some people feel more comfortable with things being left the same way; therefore, they won't have to learn how to do something differently.

Chapter 2

How Do People Keep the Spark Going in a Relationship?

Both people in the relationship have to be honest with each other and show that they trust one another. Also, by being yourself, the relationship will last a whole lot longer. Honesty is a virtue that is required to keep any relationship going. If you hide the person you really are and it comes out during your relationship, it is not guaranteed that your relationship will last.

Some people feel that sex, dates, more sex, and surprises keep the spark going in a relationship. First off, sexual activity usually is required, but a whole bunch seems like too much. One may begin to believe that is all their significant other is there for. Going out on dates is good because it is showing that you care and spending time with your significant other at the same time.

By surprising your significant other, they never know what to expect, so in other words, you keep them guessing. Some people believe a person can keep the spark going in a relationship by communication sex. Even though a couple may have been together for a while, it won't hurt to still flirt every now and again with each other. Some people believe in keeping things new, because nobody likes the same old same old.

Basically, you have to change things up every once in a while, because doing the same things repeatedly may turn into a bore. Also, showing your significant other affection on the regular will let them know they still interest you. If there's never a time their significant other wants to have sexual activity with them, the person may begin to feel there's no love there anymore. Some people believe that gifts, flowers, and candy can keep the spark going in a relationship.

In a relationship, it is good at times to buy something for your person showing that you care. Some people believe to keep the spark going in a relationship, there must be great sex. Basically, both people in the relationship need to be enjoying the sexual intercourse, or their attention could easily turn elsewhere. Another way to keep the spark going in a relationship is by not only thinking about yourself.

A relationship is like a two-way street. In order to keep a relationship going right, both people must not stay on one side of the street always. In order to keep the spark going in a relationship, both people should do the things they did when they first met, such as flirting and things. Usually the same things it takes to get the person are the same things it take to keep the person.

By making sure the other person keeps a smile, someone can keep the spark going in a relationship. If you are making sure your significant other is smiling every day, you feel they are happy, so basically you are doing one job right in your relationship. In order to keep the spark going in a relationship, people have to learn how to show each other love. If both people in a relationship love each other, making each other happy should come naturally.

Usually when they learn to show each other love, they have already learned their person's personality. By running bathwater for your significant other and being straight with them, you can keep the spark going in a relationship. Running bathwater for your partner is one of those small things that may mean a lot. Even though it may not seem like much, it's the thought that counts.

Honesty is a virtue that counts greatly in a relationship. No matter how bad the situation may seem, people should always tell the truth in a relationship.

Chapter 3

Why Do People Turn Gay/Lesbian?

Some believe the females may have gotten tired of men because they were never treated right; the males are believed to be sick. Bad relationships are one of the main reasons why some people give up on dating the opposite sex and turn to the same sex. There are some people who feel like they don't want the opposite sex anymore, so maybe they want to try something new. Sometimes some people have these different feelings or empty places inside of them and they want to find out the reason.

Some people believe that males may have been abused when they were little, did not have a father figure, or they were raped by a man. If a child is being abused, there is really nothing they can do about it. The child may wonder why, but as for trying to get help, they may be too afraid or either confused about how. There are some males who never had a male role model in their life to be an influence for them.

With only their mother around, all the male had was an influence from a female. A rape is forced, so if a male was constantly getting raped by a man when they were younger, they might get used to it after a while and decide that's what they want to be with. Some people think the person who turns was always that way and just came out of the closet. Those feelings the person kept locked away, telling them they were not what they were supposed to be, got so strong that they had to be acted on and released.

Some people turn gay/lesbian because they have been hurt so badly that they don't trust the opposite sex. So basically the person knew they probably shouldn't go with the same sex, but since they had gotten hurt so badly by the opposite sex, they did not want to take any more chances. Another reason is because they don't feel wanted by the other sex, and when they get around the same sex it makes them feel more comfortable. Some people try so hard to get attention from the opposite sex and still get denied.

When the same sex shows them some attention, they get an accepted feeling, and obviously they like the way it feel. Some people turn gay/lesbian because they can't find someone of the opposite sex, so they feel they have no choice but to turn to someone of the same sex. Obviously, the person who turns never could find their perfect match, and since they don't want to be alone, they would rather try to find their match in someone of the same sex. Past abusive relationships may also cause someone to turn gay/lesbian.

Neither sex wants to be hurt or mistreated, but they especially do not want to be abused. If the opposite sex keeps on hurting them physically, the person may begin to think of the same sex as better because they won't abuse them. There are some people who believe that people turn because it's not really a choice; it's the way the person was born. It all deals with those inside feelings people have.

Everyone usually trusts their feelings and most likely their feelings will lead them to the choice they make. No one is born gay/lesbian; it's something that comes from when hormones kick in later on. Babies are born clueless; they have to learn everything, so they have no idea what gay/lesbian is. Some people may have been mentally hurt by the opposite sex.

In the person's mind, their feelings may have gotten so twisted up and confused because of the opposite sex that they would rather deal with the same sex. Some people may turn gay/lesbian because of something that started off when they were kids at slumber parties and by playing "truth or dare" games. At slumber parties, people try doing anything that seems like fun. In the game "truth or dare," nobody likes turning down a dare, and you can dare somebody to do anything.

Chapter 4

Why Are People Afraid of Commitment?

Some people are afraid of commitment because they don't want to get hurt. They feel if they commit to someone, everything in their relationship will change. Sometimes people don't find out a person's true color until they commit to them. Some people feel they can't be satisfied with just one person.

Obviously when this person is dating someone, they still are attracted to other people. Some people feel they don't want to be in one relationship forever because they will feel trapped. One may feel they won't have as much free time as they used to. Some people don't want to risk their heart getting broken, while others don't want to deal with the feelings or emotions.

Everyone is afraid of getting hurt, but when you actually get your heart broken, it is hard to trust anyone again. When you commit to someone, you have different feelings and emotions. They can be either weak or strong, and sometimes they can overwhelm you. Some people believe people in a relationship are afraid of commitment because they don't want to take on responsibility.

When someone commits to another person, everything has turned into an equal partnership; therefore, it is ultimately both people's job to make the relationship work. Some people are afraid of commitment because they don't have confidence in themselves or their partners. If someone in a relationship has it in their head that they won't make it, then most likely they won't because that is what they believe. If a person commits to someone and feelings change, they don't want to be burdened, so if they don't commit, they don't have to worry about all of it.

Sometimes a person in a relationship may feel strongly about their significant other and believe they can spend the rest of their life with them. But then they realize their feelings for the person are not as strong as they thought they were. The person may begin to think their significant other is nothing other than a burden. So in other words, if they don't commit, they don't have to worry about all of it.

Some people are afraid of commitment because they feel like they are missing out on something. Obviously one person in the relationship begins to feel there is someone else out there they may be attracted to. Some people feel as if they are not free because their partner may want to be in control and they don't want to be controlled. If one person wants to be in control all the time in a relationship, the other person will begin to feel like they are living in a dictatorship.

Even though they may not own up to it, some people are afraid of being with the same person for many years. Some people believe if they are in a relationship for a long time, the person will grow tired of them and change in how they are treating them.

Chapter 5

Why Are There So Many Disagreements in Relationships?

Some people believe there are so many disagreements in relationships because the females never want to be wrong. Regardless of who's wrong or right, it still stands; no compromise has been reached. Some people are not really made for each other. Then, there are those people who are just in a relationship for comfort.

At times, when people first start a relationship, they believe it will last forever, but sometimes feelings change. Sometimes people are in a relationship because they don't think they can handle being alone. Some people believe people don't have to agree to an opinion in relationships, but it's necessary to. Sometimes in a relationship, a person may say something just to be saying it and expect you to agree, and when you don't it turns into a disagreement.

Some people believe there are so many disagreements in relationships because people have different backgrounds and beliefs. People feel strongly for what they believe in, and you never know what someone has been through. If you share your doubts to something that someone believe strongly in, you can hurt them a whole lot more than you know. Some people believe there are so many disagreements in

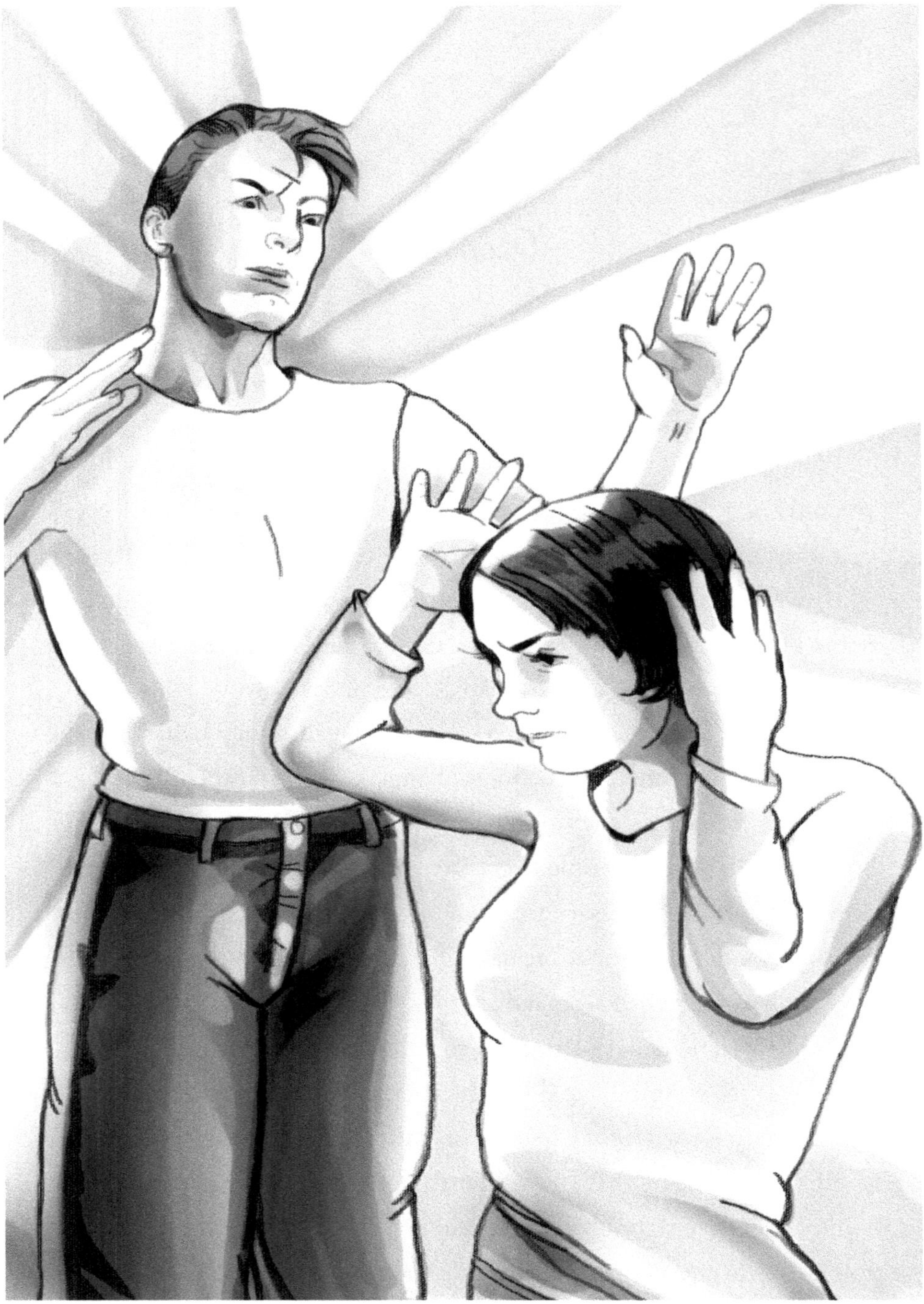

relationships because a relationship involves two different people, so there are always two different sides to a situation.

Sometimes both people may know and understand something, but they accept it and understand it differently. Sometimes one person in the relationship just wants to make the other person mad on purpose. Maybe they feel an even stronger attraction to the person when they make them angry. If the person did not care about them, they probably would not care what they said or did.

Some people don't know how to communicate or the couple just grows apart. Communication is one of the keys to a lasting relationship. Talking to each other will help a couple understand each other better. When a couple grows apart, that means their feelings for each other have changed.

Usually when something like that happens, it is best to end the relationship before both people start to hate each other. People in relationships must realize they are not going to find somebody that agrees with everything. To be right about every single thing, that would give someone a quality of being perfect, and no one is completely perfect. Even if the person in a relationship was right most of the time, that still doesn't mean the other person has to agree to what they were right about.

Some people believe there are so many disagreements in relationships because two people don't know each other like they should and they have not learned each other. There are some people who hook up with another person because of the way they look instead of trying to learn the person's personality. If they don't learn each other's ways or personality, they will have many disagreements and eventually they will break up. People have likes and dislikes.

Basically everyone is not always going to like and dislike the same things. Of course, "all men are created equal," but they all were entitled to their own opinion.

Chapter 6

Why Would Someone Get Bored with Their Significant Other in a Relationship?

Their significant other may keep doing the same thing over and over and they get tired. Some people like to try different things. If someone keeps on doing the same thing over and over, it will quickly and easily get on their nerves. Someone would get bored with their significant other because things have started to feel different.

Although it may not seem like it, people can tell when someone they care about starts treating them different. Even though they are not showing it, they are probably extremely hurt. They may begin to feel unappreciated and unloved. Another reason someone would get bored with their significant other is because someone else has caught their eye.

Some people date a person and may decide too soon that they want to be with them only. Then they happen to see this other person, who is a whole lot more interesting than the person they are with. Someone will get bored with their significant other if they are looking for something different. So basically the person they are with is nothing but a rebound mate.

When they find somebody they actually like, they will leave the person they are with anyway. Someone will also get bored with their significant other if they're not spending enough time together or spending time together, but not spending time together. Basically, if their significant other is always gone, the person will start to feel lonely. Sometimes the person may be home with them but is not talking to them or acknowledging their presence, so they might as well not be there.

Another reason someone would get bored with their significant other is because of the sex. Maybe the sex does not feel as good as it should to them. Obviously, they believe there is someone out there who can do a whole lot better. Some people believe it's because relationships are lame.

They believe relationships are too old fashioned and feel tied down when they are in a relationship. Sometimes people do things too many times in a relationship and don't try to spice things up. If someone is going to keep on doing the same thing, they can at least do something new with it each time and keep it from getting old and boring. Another reason is because their significant other is not showing them any love.

Lack of attention from their partner can have something to do with it. Then, it could be because their partner doesn't take them anywhere or buy them anything. Some people are not compatible, bored with each other, or they just have been together too long. In some cases, relationships are just not meant to be.

Basically, they are like two gloves that are not a match. Some people may act too much alike, so without there being anything different in the relationship, the couple will soon get bored with each other. Although the couple in a relationship may still act the same, they may find themselves arguing or fighting too much of the time after a long period of time. Being together too much of the time and too long can cause a couple to grow apart if they are not separate at least sometimes.

The people in the relationship may get bored with each other if they don't do anything together, or they may just be tired of their person. People will get tired of just sitting around doing nothing all the time. Being in a relationship, they feel they should at least get out and have a little fun sometimes. If they are just tired of the person they are with, maybe the relationship has reached its course.

Every relationship is not meant to last, so if one person is tired of the other person, maybe they should just go ahead and end the relationship before they start hating the person. Attitudes can cause a person to get bored with their significant other. Sometimes, even if you do everything you possibly can, you still can't impress some people. When you get tired of trying, it will become somewhat of a bore, and most likely you will go to try to impress someone else.

Some people might get used to their person, or get confused about how to spark new things. After being around someone for a long time, people in relationships have grown to know each other very well. It may seem hard to spark new things because everything has already been tried. Over time, people in relationships may become unattractive to their person because they have gotten older and they see younger people.

Their person may look different now in their eyes, and the younger person may look how their person used to look. Then, they may get it in their head that they may feel younger if they are with a younger person. Some people in a relationship stop doing what they used to do for their person. Some people don't realize the same thing it took to get the person is the same thing it takes to keep the person.

They feel that since they already have you, they don't have to go all out trying to impress you.

Chapter 7

What's the Number-One Mistake People Make When They Have a Good Person?

Some people believe the number-one mistake people make when they have a good person is telling other people too much information about their relationship. Although you may not know it, someone you call your friend could be sitting back waiting on their chance to get the person you are with. They are just sitting there, listening to everything you say and getting to know the person through you. Other people believe the number-one mistake people make when they have a good person is taking that person for granted.

If one person in the relationship does certain things to impress their significant other, the other person will start expecting them to do those things, as if they don't have any choice about it. Another mistake people make when they have a good person is taking advantage of them. They are commanding the person to do things just because they know the person will. Some people leave a person for somebody bad.

People usually don't realize they have something good until it's gone. Obviously, the person doesn't like the person who is treating them well because they are so used to someone treating them badly. Other people think about past relationships and try to apply them to the relationship they are in. Some people feel the new relationship they start will be the same as their last, without thinking of the fact that all people are different.

Even though all men are created the same, they have different personalities and beliefs. Cheating is another mistake people make when they have a good person. Fear of being in a new relationship can cause a person to cheat. The person may have been in a relationship before and gotten hurt, so they cheat so that if they get hurt, they might not be hurt as badly.

They are also confused about what they are supposed to do and what they are not supposed to do because the relationship seems too good to be true. Then, they may feel they are falling in love too fast and are afraid of being hurt. Some people do dumb things, such as lie, cheat, and steal people's hearts. The person may have been raised wrong and doesn't know how to treat people.

Some people may do it because they think it's fun to hurt someone who cares about them. Some people distrust the person they are with too much. Basically, if the person is accused of doing something they are not doing too often, it will make them want to do it because they are already being accused. People tend to cheat because they know the good person won't want to leave; they will want to at least talk about it first.

They feel that since the person will be there anyway, they can do whatever they want. Talking things out usually helps a relationship, but if the other person doesn't really care, then talking won't help. Some people take their significant other for granted, thinking they will always be there, knowing that being in a relationship, they are supposed to be there for each other. When a woman and a man love each other, they battle over who can do the most.

Sometimes instead of both people being there for each other in a relationship, one person feels they need all the attention and the other person doesn't really need any. A couple who truly cares about each other does not think about themselves first. Some people lust and forget what they have at home. Even though a person may love their significant other, they may find they are still sexually attracted to other people.

When they are having these sexual feelings about this other person, their loved one is not on their mind. Some people cheat because they don't know what they have until they lose it. They feel they can do whatever they want and still keep the person they have. Hurting the other person's feelings does not cross their mind, and they don't care as long as they get their way.

Having expectations is another mistake people make when they have a good person. Basically, one person should not expect too much from another person. When you expect too much, you will get hurt. If you don't expect too much from someone, when they do something it won't surprise you to the point of breaking you down.

Chapter 8

Do You Think It Is Necessary to Lie to Your Significant Other?

No. Because if you're honest like you say you're honest, and you trust each other like you say you trust each other, then you should have no reason to lie to each other. Basically, if you feel you have to lie to your significant other, the question "How much do you really care about them?" should form. Keeping secrets and being dishonest are two reasons why relationships fail.

Yes. Because some people have more than one person. Technically speaking, there are only supposed to be two people in a relationship. Those two are you and your significant other. Because even if the people have an open relationship, they are honest with each other about whom they invite in.

Sometimes. So that you won't hurt the person's feelings. Like, if your significant other spent hours in the kitchen cooking, and when you eat it, it is not very good, you might say it is to spare their feelings. If you didn't care, you would tell them the truth, knowing they would get upset but not caring.

No. Because you have to have honesty to build, and that's the foundation of a relationship. You can't start a relationship and keep it going based on a lie. People can't build anything lying because there won't be any trust behind anything they do or say to each other.

No. Because a relationship is based on trust, honesty, and faith; if you don't have that, you're not being honest with yourself. If people believe their relationship will work, then most likely it will. But if they go around doubting the relationship, and not putting any effort to make it work, then most likely it will fail.

No. Because you don't want them lying to you. The person doing the lying doesn't think about how it would make the other person feel. Basically, if they think about how it would make them feel, they could conclude how it would make the other person feel.

Sometimes. Because their significant other can make things bigger than they really are, so if they don't say anything they can avoid conflicts. Some people take things harder than others, so to protect their feelings, it is better to leave some things unsaid.

No. Because you shouldn't have to lie. A relationship is based on trust, so if you have to lie, there is no trust. So that means the person may be doing something they have no business doing.

No. Because if you feel the person is your other half, you should be able to tell them anything and they not take it the wrong way. Talking things through always helps a couple to reach an agreement. If you trust your partner, you can talk to them about anything without worrying about them getting angry or taking things the wrong way.

It depends. Because if it's something that's going to make the person mad or something they don't need to know, then just don't tell them. To spare the person's feelings, it's better not to tell them the truth all the time. Then, if you feel it is nothing they need to know, you might just keep it to yourself anyway. If only you know, and you feel it's not important, there is no point asking the other person.

No. Because you have to keep lying and you will eventually get caught. When a person lies, they have to lie again to cover up, and then most likely they will forget what the lie was that they told the first time.

Sometimes. It depends on what the person is lying about. To spare a person's feelings, you may conclude that it is better to not tell them the truth. But some people would rather have an honest opinion, no matter if it would hurt them or not.

No. To stay in a relationship that is serious, lying would not be one of the requirements.

No. Why would someone want to be in a relationship with lies? The relationship won't get anywhere if it's full of lies. Some people would rather deal with lies than deal with the truth. The truth may hurt them a lot more than the lie.

No. If someone truly loves their person, then the problem can be worked around. The person should not even consider lying when a problem comes up. If they have to lie, they didn't trust that their person would understand and listen.

Chapter 9

How Do You Think You Would Feel if You Were the One Being Ignored in a Relationship?

Some people would feel alone and begin to think they might as well be by themselves. If a person in a relationship is being ignored, they will start thinking that maybe they shouldn't be in the relationship at all. Since they feel they are by themselves, they might as well be. Others who wouldn't like it would eventually try to seek attention from somebody else.

Why waste time trying to get attention of the person they are with, when there is someone out there who would love their attention? If the person they are with doesn't show them the attention they need, they can go to the person who will. Some people would feel hurt that they are not wanted anymore and would wonder why. Even though the person who is ignoring them seems not to care, that doesn't mean the feelings of the person being ignored have changed for them.

They still care for that person and wonder why that person is treating them the way they are. If problems have occurred in the relationship, they feel there should be a way to fix them. Others would feel like something else is going on. Since their significant other is ignoring them, their attention must be going to somebody else.

Obviously since they are not paying them any attention, their mind must be on something or someone besides them. Since everyone wants attention, some people would probably feel like they need to get out of the relationship. The person being ignored wouldn't see any point in still being there. They would feel if they left, the person wouldn't even know they were gone and probably wouldn't care.

Some people would feel like the person is hiding something or they probably want their own space just to be ignored. Since the person never ignored them before, they may begin to feel like they are keeping some kind of secret they don't want them knowing about. Maybe the person doing the ignoring needs some time to themselves. They may feel like they are with their partner too much and need some time to breathe and think alone.

Others would feel like they should just forget the person and go do their own thing. Since it is obvious that their significant other doesn't want to show them attention and doesn't care, the person feels like why should they even bother still trying? Basically, if they do their own thing, their significant other still won't notice. Some people would try to abuse the person ignoring them.

They would most likely get to a point where they are way past understanding. Tired of being on an emotional ride and being hurt, they will try to make the person show them attention. Others would get mad, because you're supposed to talk when someone is talking to you. When someone is expressing how they feel, they expect their significant other to acknowledge them.

If they still ignore them, they feel as if they wasted their time talking in the first place. Why talk to someone who couldn't really care less about how they feel? Some people might get mad and bring it up, hoping their significant other might do something to acknowledge they are there. By the time they bring it up, they have been putting up with the lack of attention for a long time.

They feel if they bring it up, they may finally get their significant other to pay attention to them.

Chapter 10

Why Do People Feel It Is Necessary to Have Sex before Marriage?

Some people have insecurities and feel it will make the person like them more. Because some people are insecure, they will do whatever it takes to keep the person they care about. In their mind, they think the person feels for them the same way when they actually don't. A lot of people want to sample things before they buy them. Most people probably don't want to be stuck with bad sex for the rest of their life.

People see things that might be good and want to buy them, even though they are not sure. It could be bad or it could be good, but you never know if you choose not to take a chance. Marriage is something that is meant to last a lifetime. If you get married and the sex is bad, it will be too late to call it quits.

Some people want to see how it feels. Curiosity leads people to want to see how it feels to have sex. Does it hurt or does it feel good? They feel they are a long way from getting married and think, what would it hurt to try this one thing just once?

It's just something that's been going on for generations. Obviously years ago, people stopped believing in waiting until they got married to have sex. They feel marriage is just too strong of a commitment to wait for and that it's really not promised to all people. Some females may be trying to find a father figure by sleeping with a man.

Their father may have never been around, so they get really happy and excited when a male shows them any attention at all. A lot of people confuse infatuation with love. Some people may think they love someone when it's actually just a huge crush. Then, there could be the possibility of them just wanting to be intimate with the person.

But afterward, their attention has moved somewhere else. Some people believe that's just how the world is today. Since things changed so much, most people feel saving their virtue is unimportant. Then, they notice other people giving it up, so they think, *I might as well, too.*

The other thought they have is that they may not get married anyhow. Others may want the person to stay with them and want to take it to a serious relationship. Since the person wants their body, they feel like if they give it up, they can keep the person. They don't consider the fact that could be all the person wanted them for.

Some people want to know how good the person is at sexual activity. They want to be sure the person can keep them satisfied sexually before they marry them. Being tempted by someone else will be too easy if they are unsatisfied. Some males think it is a competition and they may be trying to be cool, while females are trying to be accepted by the man.

The males feel that if they save themselves until marriage, they will get criticized and talked about, but they also want to fit in with the other males. The females feel if they give it up to the man, he will stay with them and won't want to leave. Others feel it is fun to have sex before marriage. It is obvious they enjoy the excitement and feel of it.

They don't think about the fact that sexual activity is meant to be shared with married people. Alcohol has some really bad effects. Some people get drunk and don't remember what happened after they sober down. Even though they didn't mean for something to happen, it happens and the alcohol makes them have no self-control.

Some people are just talking out of the side of their head. When you have sex before marriage, it's just dumb. Even though some people believe having sex before marriage is all right, others believe it doesn't make sense. If they wait, they will be able to give their virtue to their husband or wife as it was meant to be. Other people just want to have sex and they can't wait.

Even though being a virgin is precious, some people don't see it that way. They feel the sooner they have sex, the better. Afterward, they won't have to deal with the peer pressure of still being a virgin.

Printed in the USA
CPSIA information can be obtained
at www.ICGtesting.com
LVHW020934020424
776139LV00002B/356